50 WAYS TO WEAR ACCESSORIES

Lauren Friedman

CHRONICLE BOOKS

SAN FRANCISCO

Library of Congress Cataloging-in-Publication Data:

Names: Friedman, Lauren, 1987- author.
Title: 50 ways to wear accessories / Lauren Friedman.
Other titles: Fifty ways to wear accessories
Description: San Francisco : Chronicle Books, [2018]
Identifiers: LCCN 2017038586 | ISBN 9781452166483 (hardcover : alk. paper)
Subjects: LCSH: Dress accessories. | Women's clothing. | Fashion.
Classification: LCC TT649.8 .F75 2018 | DDC 646/.3—dc23 LC record available at https://lccn.loc.gov/2017038586

Manufactured in China

MIX
Paper from responsible sources
FSC
www.fsc.org
FSC™ C008047

Design by Jennifer Tolo Pierce
Typesetting by Howie Severson

10 9 8 7 6 5 4 3 2 1

Chronicle books and gifts are available at special quantity discounts to corporations, professional associations, literacy programs, and other organizations. For details and discount information, please contact our corporate/premiums department at corporatesales@chronicle-books.com or at 1-800-759-0190.

Chronicle Books LLC
680 Second Street
San Francisco, California 94107
www.chroniclebooks.com

To my ancestors, and those that wish to be inspired. This is also dedicated to the countless accessories I have lost over the years. You are not forgotten.

CONTENTS

INTRODUCTION

Accessories are a universal language that bridges age, language, religion, creed, and any other superficial label we apply to one another. Visit a foreign country wearing a unique pair of sunglasses or an eye-catching scarf, and you will almost certainly find an admirer who suddenly speaks the same language as you: the language of appreciation. In the span of a single afternoon while working on this book, I met a new friend thanks to our mutual admiration of one another's scarves, I gained a new perspective with someone while we bonded over our watches, and I ended up talking about God with a stranger after his compliment of my shoes sparked a conversation.

Accessories are philosophically intriguing. They have long been used as amulets, safeguards against evil, protective measures that are literally held close to the body. There is a heady enchantment in accessories that isn't found in anything else you wear. A brooch can make you feel safe, a hat can make you feel proud, a belt can make you feel ravishing. These objects, which are often passed down from family members or friends, are imbued with a sacred energy. I wear something of my grandmother Enid's, who passed away in 2015, every day. I feel as if I am simply the current generational guardian, in a long line of wearers and appreciators, of these objects: a newsboy cap, a turquoise ring, a crocodile-skin clutch. In wearing these things, I feel my grandmother protect me, guide me, adorn me. Accessories are a temporary inheritance, a gift from the past that makes a promise for the future.

Accessories are constantly reinvented, and in no other aspect of fashion are trends more fully felt. Accessories can tell a very detailed tale about the history of humankind, yet we tend to have short attention spans when it comes to these trends: The 2010s return of the '90s-era choker could refer to the 1500s' revival of the 1490s' trend of wearing a necklace snugly around the neck. Whether one chooses an accessory to blend in or stand out, the individual choice of embellishment is wildly personal. No other item we put on our bodies expresses our unique inner desires, passions, and identities, nor tells a story of history, like the accessory.

Styles may cycle, and tastes may differ, but the truth is that humans have always expressed themselves through accessories. In the process of writing and illustrating this book, I noted with a fresh appreciation that in every school photo through twelfth grade, I'm wearing a constantly changing *parure* (set) of accessories—the passage of time marked not just by my growth and my gummy smile transformed by braces, but also by the evolution of my accessory choices. Unchanging, nonetheless, was the importance I placed on this annual declaration of self in front of the camera for the yearbook, even in my first year in school as a kindergartener. Hair neatly combed, sporting a purple cotton scoop-neck dress covered in bright flowers, I accessorized with a handmade beaded necklace and clip-on earrings made from tiny green glass leaves (pierced ears wouldn't come until fourth grade).

I can safely say that this book, the third installment in the 50 Ways series, is the most personal. It became clear to me that I was the steward, the temporary owner, of my accessories. Many (most) of these pieces were passed down from my mom and grandmother, or gifted from friends or clients. These pieces came pre-loved, so to speak, and by immortalizing them in this book through words and pictures, I have given them the gift of eternity, of timelessness. I made a point to include as many of my own accessories in here as I could. You may see items repeated (including some items featured in my past books!), because it was important to me that I showed the hard-working versatility of my own favorite accessories. They're all in here—the necklace gifted from a friend after its previous life as part of the superhero costume in a summer camp play, the orange knit scarf I bought on an eighth-grade French class trip to Montreal, the gold letter _F_ brooch I unearthed in my grandma Enid's closet.

What I hope this book will show you is that getting dressed can be simple if you rely on a formula for putting on clothes. Even if you're wearing the same thing, such as a black dress, a few days in a row, there is a quick magic in being able to completely transform a look simply by switching out the accessories. Personally, I—never having met a blazer I didn't like—turn to a closet of jackets, button-up shirts, and vintage tees, paired with slim jeans or high-rise skirts. Although I am relatively obdurate about wearing unfussy black, white, gray, and blue clothes, I've amassed, over the years, a set of reliable splashes, to wit, a happy red, which appears on a purse, belts in different widths, slip-on loafers, and sandals; a royal blue, featured on pairs of wedges, heels, and flats; and a warm burgundy, found on numerous scarves, a handbag, and a pair of leather boots. I also have a hard time saying no to an animal print accessory! However you feel comfortable getting dressed, and no matter what styles you enjoy wearing most, I encourage you to start paying attention to the accessories that speak to your deepest inner visions and desires. Getting dressed becomes easy, as everything "goes together" effortlessly for the simple, pure fact that you adore everything you're adorning yourself with. The advice here is not necessarily to buy new things but to commit to the things you already own and love.

Sure, maybe some of the suggestions in this book seem wacky or a little crazy for your every day. But why not reach for the beloved objects that would thrill to be worn on a Tuesday morning or a Saturday evening? It's audacious yet intentional. The worst thing that could happen is these embellishments will shine so brightly that everyone will notice. That's the beauty of accessories—they speak to your deepest heart's desire, an outer reflection of your inner beauty. So go ahead, pin a brooch on your winter hat. Bring your evening clutch to brunch. Utilize your accessories to outwardly express how you inwardly feel. My hope is to inspire you to turn to your jewelry box, your pile of handbags, your drawer of belts, and be inspired to wear these items in new ways. Commit to their exalted place in your life and your wardrobe. Who knows where they could take you, and whom you could meet by wearing them. However you choose to wear them, wear them with feeling!

CARING FOR YOUR ACCESSORIES

Your jewelry should be the last thing you put on and the first thing you take off. Avoid using aerosols or lotions while wearing your jewelry. The safest way to clean most jewelry is with warm water and gentle soap, applied gently with a soft toothbrush. However, porous gemstones such as coral, turquoise, and pearls should be kept away from all abrasive chemicals, including soap. To remove dust or debris from your tender gemstones, wipe clean with a damp soft cloth. And most important, avoid cleaning your jewelry near an open drain in the sink!

Use only professional lens cleaner for cleaning your glasses—household cleaners can be abrasive to certain lens coatings. Use a designated

lens wipe instead of your shirt or another fabric, which could contain small debris and scratch your lenses. Wash the cloth lens wipe every few weeks; you can just throw it in with your laundry.

When removing your glasses, take them off with two hands so that the temples don't stretch unevenly. Keep away from damaging aerosols, like hairspray and other chemicals.

Make a practice of emptying your handbag regularly (this is easier if you employ small clutches for various items that you can easily switch between bags). Then wipe the inside and outside clean with a cloth or tissue before putting it away. You can also help extend the life of your handbags by avoiding setting them on floors in public spaces.

STORING YOUR ACCESSORIES

Organize your accessories by color so you can find everything at a glance. A small handbag can fit tidily inside a larger, similarly toned bag—make sure the handles of the small bag are hanging outside the opening of the larger bag so you don't forget where it lives. Store bags and other accessories away from direct sunlight and harsh chemicals.

Neat trays made from soft materials such as felt, fabric, or leather keep your jewelry safe from scratches and your necklaces tangle-free. You could also hang your necklaces from individual *S*-hooks to keep them from becoming a snarled heap.

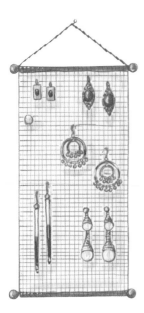

Your accessories can double as décor as long as they are safe from the glare of harsh sunlight. For example, an earring holder displays your favorite pieces and makes picking a pair a breeze.

Belts can be hung from a tie hanger so you can see and access them all effortlessly.

Keep your seasonal items, like sunglasses or heavy scarves, within easy grabbing distance when you're on the go so that you don't forget to wear them.

THE LOOKS

THE
~FROSTING~

HOW TO WEAR EARRINGS

Like the flourish of a whipped topping on a delicious cake, a pair of earrings are the sweetest finish to whatever look you're trying to complete. Whether your ears are pierced or not, every visage deserves a final sugary touch.

TIP: Don't have your ears pierced? No problem! A pair of clip-on earrings can be a low-commitment way of introducing sparkle to your look. Look for pairs that sit comfortably on the lobe without too much pinching or pulling.

Earrings are the jewelry you wear closest to your face, so consider these recommendations when adorning your lobes.

No matter the style, matching your earrings to your eye color makes your whole face sing.

Small earrings are a quiet, classic statement that work for plenty of occasions, including day wear, conservative workplaces, and minimalist fancy events,

while big statement earrings are for when you feel bold.

Geometric shapes add modern panache,

while wearing a single earring proves that a little asymmetry can be intriguing.

Or, mix it up by slipping on mismatching earrings. (Many people have one ear that sits higher than the other. Hang your longer earring on your higher ear for a bit of balance amidst the differentiation.)

THE
NORTHERN
❧ LIGHTS ❧

HOW TO WEAR HAIR ACCESSORIES

For as long as humans have had hair, we have decorated our domes with any number of unique, sky-lighting accessories. Just like the flash of the aurora borealis through the night sky, a hair accessory, whether streamlined or extravagant, is an out-of-this-world, heavenly touch.

For a spectacular view, embellish your hair with any of these noteworthy additions.

Layer a headband over a scarf.

Clip on a barrette (or simply layer a collection of bobby pins), angled just above one ear. For the most flattering placement, clip your barrette at the hairline above your temple, angled toward the highest point of your eyebrow.

Get a little crafty and glue something interesting, such as tiny bows, pearls, or small figurines, to the ends of bobby pins and disperse throughout your updo.

On the back of your head . . .

. . . a pretty bracelet can moonlight as a hair accessory. After styling your hair in a half updo, slip bobby pins through the ends of each side of the bracelet and then secure beneath your updo . . .

add interest to a ponytail with a unique scrunchie, like one in faux fur,

or wear a brooch in your hair, below a ballerina bun, as pictured here, or pinch-hitting as a barrette embellishing a half-up updo. Secure it with a bobby pin inserted below the bar pin.

THE

Catch of the Day

HOW TO PICK OUT GLASSES

When it comes to reeling in a charming look for your face, no other accessory combines such form and function as a pair of glasses. No matter what kind of style pond you like to fish from, an appealing pair of specs is always a good item with which to bait your hook.

As a general guideline, choose a style of glasses that have a different shape than your face. For instance . . .

. . . round faces look great in square glasses,

while square faces look smashing in round glasses.

Heart-shaped faces are lovely in cat-eye specs or frames that taper at the temples,

and oval-shaped faces look good in any style.

Try on everything, use a handheld mirror, and check yourself out in different lights— inside and out.

Glasses are, after all, an accessory! If your budget allows, consider picking out two pairs so that you can select your specs according to mood and setting.

TIP: Embrace the functionality and the bonus style points of a glasses keeper to keep your frames fashionably at bay.

THE
SPOTLIGHT
✳ KEEPER ✳

HOW TO WEAR MAKEUP
AS AN ACCESSORY

Makeup doesn't have to be a corrective measure to cover up supposed "flaws." By employing hues on your face the way you would use a pop of color in a handbag or belt, you'll always be ready for the limelight.

Here are some fun ways to use lipstick as a colorful accessory.

Consider matching your lip color to an element in your outfit.

Mixing two lipstick shades is guaranteed to produce a more flattering shade. Try it to add color to a monochromatic outfit, like denim on denim.

Lipstick isn't just for the lips. For a monochromatic look on your face, swipe a flattering shade on your lips, blend it on your cheeks as a blush, and apply a small amount to the corners of your eyelids as a cream shadow.

And there are other fun ways to introduce color to your visage.

A colored mascara is a subtle yet enticing way to introduce a different tone to your look. Try matching it to a pair of earrings.

Or, instead of earrings, apply a glitter eye shadow or highlighting cream to your earlobes, which will throw a flattering glow onto your profile.

THE
Made in the Shade

HOW TO WEAR A HAT IN HOT WEATHER

A cool cover from hot rays may be the ultimate luxury on a sunny day. The opportunities are ripe for donning something spectacular yet functional.

Play up the fashion while shielding from sun damage by . . .

. . . tying a scarf around the band of a hat for an updated look,

or wrapping a scarf around your head before putting on a wide straw hat for added style and to keep you from getting sweaty.

A bucket hat looks well loved when a collection of pins are placed jauntily on the sides,

and a statement brooch smack-dab in the middle of a baseball cap proves you root for your own.

Hair worn in a messy bun off to one side works with all types of toppers,

and two braids also look great with any warm-weather hat.

THE

⁕ UNLIKELY HERO ⁕

HOW TO WEAR A HAT
IN COLD WEATHER

When battling frigid climes, a chapeau does double duty: It protects from cold and wet elements while allowing you to seize the moment and be daring among a sea of gray beanies.

TIP: To outsmart hat hair, flip your hair to the opposite side of where you normally part your hair before putting on your hat. Then when you take off your hat, shake out your hair and return it to your usual style.

Stay warm with these cold-weather suggestions.

In chilly weather, your hat doesn't have to be slouchy. Look for a hat made from a long-lasting material such as wool or cashmere for day-to-day use, and be sure to consider how it goes with your good winter coat.

A faux fur hat commands respect in frigid or dressed-up conditions, while keeping you exceptionally warm.

A hat with a pom-pom adds cheer to plenty of activities, especially playing in the snow.

When considering your hair under these cold-weather toppers, keep the following in mind:

Earmuffs keep your ears warm while preserving an updo.

With a felt fedora, tuck your hair into a scarf or sweater to protect it from harsh weather. Match your hat to a scarf in a similar color but different texture or pattern.

Pigtails or two braids are a classic, sporty way to wear your hair with a hat.

7

THE
TRIPLE
CROWN

HOW TO DRESS UP WITH A HAT

You'll win all the races with a formal topper! Come out of the gates boldly by choosing something spectacular to top your dressy look.

Consider some of these ideas when putting together a formal outfit:

Match the color of your hat to your outfit, such as this cloche and suit.

Wear a wide-brimmed hat and your favorite celebration dress to a formal daytime event.

Rock a statement-making headpiece with a gown and glamorous accessories.

8

THE
Carmencita

HOW TO ACCESSORIZE WITH FLOWERS

What is it about a bloom near the face that instantly adds a fierce yet feminine air? Whether you reach for real or fake, flowers are a lush touch.

There are as many ways to accessorize with flowers as there are botanical species. Here are some ways to start budding:

Tuck a large single bloom, such as a lily, behind one ear and secure with a bobby pin.

Arrange tiny flowers, like bits of lavender, around a bun (or two).

Weave small flowers, like ranunculus, into braids.

Make a daisy chain halo and wear with wild curls.

A floral crown made of big blooms, like roses, makes a major impact.

One large bloom, like this hydrangea, tucked into a head wrap is all you need to turn heads.

TIP: A flower in a buttonhole is a low-risk way to incorporate blossoms into your look. Secure with a safety pin.

9

THE
HEAD OF
THE CLASS

HOW TO WEAR A NECKLACE

A necklace is always a
go-to style choice, for
good reason. Stand
tall in front of the pack
with something wonderful
swinging from your neck.

You'll get top marks for style if you follow these necklace suggestions:

A choker necklace with a crew-neck shirt,

a collar necklace with a strapless top or under the lapels of a fully buttoned button-up,

a princess necklace with a scoop-neck,

a matinee necklace with a V-neck top,

an opera-length necklace or pendant with a boat-neck shirt,

or a rope or lariat necklace with a turtleneck.

TIP: Want to layer more than one necklace? Clip the clasp of one necklace to the ring of the other necklace you want to use. Forming one long loop, wrap it around your neck twice for a layered look without the tangles.

10

THE

Queen Bee

HOW TO WEAR A BROOCH

A brooch may be the most versatile yet underappreciated type of trinket in your jewelry box. Employ one or many, but be prepared for the whole hive to follow suit!

TIP: Consider this when you're fastening a brooch to the breast of jacket, coat, dress, or top: Are you leaving your physical heart covered or open? A brooch can act as a shield if you wear it on the left. If you want to lead with your heart open, fasten on the opposite side.

Pin a brooch (or five) in one of these ways, or try out your own ideas! Consider . . .

. . . pinning one on the lapel or breast of a coat or jacket for added sparkle,

fastening a small collection to one side of a dress,

using a brooch to pinch and gather fabric around the collar of a shirt or dress for a new take on the neckline,

sticking a brooch in the center of a shirt just below the collar,

pinning a small brooch on the lapel of a crisp shirt collar,

or fastening two sides of a cardigan or shirt with a brooch, either at the breastplate or above your belly button.

11

THE

(Brilliant Sun Rising)

HOW TO WEAR MULTIPLE BRACELETS

One bracelet kept in orbit around your wrist is a simple way to dress up an outfit, but an encircling stack of baubles, whether small or big, up your arm is as bright and buoyant as a new day.

On both wrists or one . . .

. . . stacks of mod bangles make a strong statement with a neutral outfit,

while a few friendship bracelets and seed beads tell a personal tale.

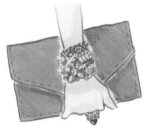

A collection of ultra-sparkly, special bracelets add flash for a formal night out,

while a combination of cuffs, bangles, and bracelets united by a common theme, be it color, time period, or style, will always speak of a unique perspective, no matter the time of day.

TIP: For an extra layer, try tying a small scarf around your wrist and clasping a bracelet on top.

12

THE
⊙TIMEPIECE⊙

HOW TO WEAR A WATCH

Whether you consider the hours
linear or circuitous, a watch is
a most useful yet classic way to
decorate the wrist.

TIP: Feeling the look of
a pocket watch but don't
want to spring for one?
Wrap a necklace around the
button of a vest, jacket, or
shirt and then tuck the end
into the nearest pocket to
create a faux watch chain.
You can secure the jewelry
by using a safety pin to
fasten it inside the pocket.

There's a perfect watch to make any outfit chime:

A no-frills metal watch, which can go with all your daily getups,

a watch with a leather strap, which looks especially dapper when worn over the cuff of an ironed shirt,

an athletic watch, which is great for both workouts and to add a sporty touch to your outfit,

or a dressy watch, which is an elegant way to add panache to an evening look.

TIP: Is your heart in another time zone? Honor a distant beloved friend, city, or country by wearing two watches, one set to where you are, one set to where your love lives.

13

THE

DESERT ROSE

HOW TO WEAR RINGS

A ring springs from your fingers like a flower amid the sand. Your hands are one of the most expressive parts of you—add a flourish to every tale with a ring!

TIP: Have a too-small ring? Try wearing it halfway down your finger, between the knuckles. Combine with other rings for a layered look.

Each finger has a different personality and begs for a different type of ring. Consider these guidelines, whether you choose one or all of them:

On your index finger, a thin sparkly band can be elegant,

while a chunky ring on the middle finger is impactful.

On your ring finger, a cameo ring gives off a debonair grace,

a ring on the pinky finger adds a fun flash,

while a thumb ring is positively bold.

14

THE
PARLOR
❧ GAMES ❧

HOW TO WEAR GLOVES

Gloves used to be de rigueur for most social situations, both in the home and out in the world. Why not play with some old-school fashion conventions and bring gloves into the present?

DID YOU KNOW?
Queen Elizabeth I, who had long, slender fingers, popularized the practice of wearing light-colored gloves that extended well beyond the fingertips as a symbol of status in the sixteenth century.

Have fun decorating your digits with gloves.

Elbow-length leather gloves solve the puzzle of what to wear with short-sleeved coats.

Driving gloves truly give you more grip on the road. Mix with iconic rubber-meets-the-road looks like a leather jacket.

Pairing lace gloves with a dress in a conservative shape is a modern take on traditional style. Slide a ring or two over your gloved fingers.

15

THE

GROUND
~SWELL~

HOW TO WEAR PEARLS

The tide always turns toward pearls when it comes to getting dressed. Pearls polish up any look and wash up a lustrous glow no matter what you're wearing.

Discover the treasure within the shell by wearing pearls some of these ways:

A single strand is lovely with a blouse, dress, or shirt—make it your signature!

A long strand of pearls can be knotted or looped twice around the neck.

A necklace featuring pearls of many shapes is right at home layered with other kinds of necklaces, including gold and silver.

A long strand can also be twisted a few times around the wrist. It's an iridescent match when paired with a gum-ball pearl cuff.

Pearl earrings add light to the face and look great on any occasion—particularly on a day when you're just wearing a simple shirt (or even sweats!).

Look for mother-of-pearl buttons to add a subtle lightness and polish to your bodice on a cardigan or shirt.

DID YOU KNOW?

The best way to heighten the luster of your pearls is to wear them. Nacre, the material created by mollusks that coats the inside of their shells and the outside of your pearls, loves the natural oils your body produces. Consider this romantic notion an invitation to take your favorite pearls for a regular spin—just be sure to have them cleaned annually by a pearl expert if you wear them daily.

16

THE
◆◆FIZZY POP◆◆

HOW TO WEAR DIAMONDS

They don't have to be real. Just be
sure they sparkle!

Diamond earrings are a fail-safe choice for every occasion. Glitter your lobes with . . .

. . . diamond studs, a
versatile choice that
goes with everything,

diamond drops, which
are as happy with a
T-shirt as a ball gown,

or diamond hoops, for the
ultimate dazzling cool.

Diamonds also twinkle . . .

. . . in a diamond ring
stacked with other rings,

in a diamond necklace
paired with a V-neck
sweater, particularly
pleasing in black, which
frames the stones
to sparkle like stars
in the night sky,

or in a diamond
bracelet that gleams as
brightly during the day
as it does at night.

17

THE
❖ Oracle ❖

HOW TO WEAR
HEIRLOOM JEWELRY

Special pieces inherited from
your ancestors should be worn
and loved. Listen to the past, be
informed by the present, and try
these new twists on ways to wear
antique bijoux.

Be creative with your heirloom pieces.

By looping a ribbon through the clasp of a vintage necklace and tying at the base of your neck, you can turn a necklace into a headband.

If a ring is too big for your fingers, loop a chain bracelet through it and connect that bracelet with another one around your wrist for your own take on hand jewelry.

A tie bar can be used as a barrette. For extra grab, apply hairspray to your hair before affixing the barrette.

A charm bracelet can be clasped to another chain to wear as a necklace.

Slip a hatpin between the buttonholes of a collar.

A brooch can be worn as a pendant on a necklace, or a dangling earring could be taken off its hook and worn as a pendant. Stud earrings could be worn as a brooch (just use the safety backs).

TIP: Keep a pair of pliers handy near your jewelry stash. That way, you can take items on and off their chains with ease.

18

THE
SPEAKEASY
✧SHIMMY✧

HOW TO WEAR A
FAUX FUR STOLE

No matter how you drape it, a faux fur stole is a versatile item in your accessory cache, imparting a louche, devil-may-care attitude reminiscent of the Roaring Twenties.

A faux fur stole can be . . .

. . . wrapped around the neck over the collar of a jacket (use a brooch to pin in place if your stole doesn't have its own fastener),

hung loose over the shoulders to give the visual impression of a vest,

draped over the crooks of your elbows,

layered over a large heavy scarf to act as a wrap,

worn underneath a jacket so that the stole peeks out,

draped over one shoulder, anchored with a statement brooch.

19

THE

~Dandy~

HOW TO WEAR A TIE

The traditional necktie is reborn as the swingingly stylish stand-in for a necklace. However you knot it, a tie will continuously convey a look of studied sophistication.

Show that you're unduly devoted to fashion by . . .

. . . wearing a loose tie with collared shirt, jacket, and pants,

knotting a tie with a crisp shirt and tucking the end into a pencil skirt, tidy cardigan optional,

or accessorizing a suit with a tie loosely knotted once against bare skin for an unconventional take on after-hours style.

TIP: Have a tiepin or tie clip? Instead of knotting your tie, let it hang from around your neck and then overlap the ends, securing with your pin or clip.

20

THE
ROCKA-
~BILLY~

HOW TO ACCESSORIZE
WITH RIBBON

That simple ribbon in your
sewing kit can be a flexible
accessory, imparting a tone
of whimsy, sweetness,
or even a little bit of
nonconformity with
a few simple ties.

To add a bow of confidence to any look . . .

. . . knot two ribbons around the collar and shoulders of a T-shirt or dress, either on the front or back side,

tie a ribbon around your neck and layer with whatever necklaces you desire, such as a pendant, collar, or choker,

wrap two long ribbons around your ankles and finish them with bows for a ballerina-inspired take with a pretty pair of shoes,

tie a ribbon over the neck of a high-collared blouse,

make a bow underneath the collar of a shirt, then layer with a cardigan, if you like,

or, for extra drama, tie a bow to hang down your back.

21

THE
DEAL MAKER

HOW TO WEAR A BELT

A belt is the finisher, the final accessory that truly ties your look together. Whether wearing one (or two!) around your hips or waist, you'll always seal the sartorial deal.

TIP: For a fun play on asymmetry, move the buckle of your belt to the side for a uniquely off-kilter look.

When wearing a belt at your waist, the most flattering spot is just below your ribs.

A wide belt at the waist creates curves no matter your shape. Consider color blocking it by matching it to either your top or your bottom.

A narrow belt is ace over a cardigan or a sheath dress.

A belt with a statement buckle, like this gold number, can act as jewelry for a pared-down look, like a black turtleneck tucked into high-waisted black pants.

It's a cinch to decorate your hips with a belt.

With a tucked-in shirt, a thin belt looped through jeans is a smooth look.

You could use a scarf as a belt, knotting it at the center or to the side.

Why not double your money? Wear two complementing belts slung around the hips.

22

THE

➤ RISE IN RANKS ◄

HOW TO WEAR A BELT WITH OUTERWEAR

A belt, the most utilitarian of accessories, is a fashion-forward recruit when worn over your coat or jacket. To sharpen the line of your outerwear is to climb to the top of the in-vogue echelons.

Spruce up your final layer with these waist-defining pairings:

A thin belt for a coat with a wide collar and volume around the shoulders (you could also swap in a shawl).

A chain link belt with a long, crisp coat, such as a chesterfield overcoat or a military-inspired trench.

A wide belt to wear over your puffiest puffer.

23

THE
Style
Wizard

HOW TO TUCK A LONG BELT

Stuck with a too-long belt?
The key to any perennially
on-point outfit is this belt tuck.
Arm yourself with a leather
hole punch and this simple
trick, and you'll find that the
accessory that used to be
relegated just to your hips
now pulls double duty around
your waist.

To employ this belt tuck . . .

1 Slip the belt around your waist and insert the belt through the belt loop, pulling completely through. You should have at least 10 to 12 in (25 to 30 cm) of excess belt length.

2 Bring the long end of the belt up behind the part of the belt that is wrapped around your waist. The tip should be pointed toward your head.

3 Loop the long end of the belt down and over the part of the belt wrapped around your waist, inserting the end through the opening you made with the previous step.

4 Pull the end all the way through and adjust as you see fit.

TIP: Invest in a leather hole punch so that you can turn your longer, hip-length belts into ones you can use on your waist. Then, employ this tuck!

24

THE
SIDECAR

HOW TO ACCESSORIZE
WITH A HANDBAG

A handbag not only carries the essentials, but also acts as a mode of communication to the outside world, conveying an intrinsic message about the wearer. Humans have carried some version of a purse since they have had things to carry in it, and its evolution has followed the arc of social mores around wealth, status, and sexuality. Choose yours wisely!

Consider these types of bags important elements that will cover all manner of personal journeys.

A medium-size bag that can be carried by the handles or worn across the shoulders is great for every day. Consider switching out a scarf tied on the handle to go with the day's outfit.

A larger bag can hold enough for a trip to the gym or a few nights of clothes. Personalize it with a hanging tag so it never gets lost in the crowd.

An evening clutch will make you ready for a Friday night dinner or a black-tie event.

A cross-body bag affords freedom of movement. Add a hanging charm or key holder for a fun extra jangle.

A statement bag, in a fun color or unique pattern, acts as a singular accessory and will brighten up any look.

A tote bag makes the perfect canvas for a collection of your favorite pins.

TIP: The easiest way to switch between purse options is to judiciously employ smaller clutches or bags that neatly envelop your essentials.

25

THE
CITY SLICKER

HOW TO ACCESSORIZE
WITH A BACKPACK

Keep your hands unrestricted by choosing a backpack and never look back! The world is your oyster when your possessions are safely tucked away in a rucksack and your hands are open to hug a friend, clutch a coffee, or carry a dog's leash. Ride free through your city with a backpack.

No matter what part of the village you hail from, a backpack looks stylish in any neighborhood.

A modern leather backpack with downtown style adds a polished urban cool to any look.

For a midtown casual getup that could include a day of sightseeing, gallery hopping, or park lounging, a slouchy patterned backpack is prime.

A sporty catchall backpack in a neutral tone goes uptown with a pencil skirt and heels for a look that flies from the gym to work to play.

26

THE

TOOTHPICK ·FAIRY·

HOW TO WEAR TIGHTS

Covering your gams with tights is not an ethereal effect—used thoughtfully, tights are a surefire way to cast a long, lean spell.

TIP: Pairing your tights with boots or closed-toe shoes? Slip on a pair of socks followed by your tights. Sounds weird, but it works amazingly well to keep you from slipping in your shoes and prolongs the life of your tights.

Bewitch and accessorize your legs with tights by choosing . . .

. . . opaque tights that match either some element of the bottom half of your outfit or your shoes (or both),

patterned tights that speak to a corresponding detail in your outfit,

colored tights that make a statement,

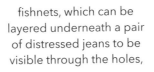

sheer tights for an immediate confidence boost (layer a sparkly anklet over one ankle for an iconoclastic take),

fishnets, which can be layered underneath a pair of distressed jeans to be visible through the holes,

or socks of any height, which can be slipped over tights when wearing open- or closed-toed shoes for a fun layered look.

27

THE

◆PIED PIPER◆

HOW TO WEAR SOCKS

Not just utilitarian, socks can be an opportunity to display a level of brashness and boldness unparalleled in your other accessories. Slip on something fun and watch others follow suit!

Decorate your feet with a merry pair of socks, like . . .

. . . striped athletic socks with sneakers,

cable-knit socks with loafers,

very fine socks with heels or wedges (extra points if they have sparkles or a fun detail around the cuffs),

funky socks with sandals,

or slip on two complementary pairs of socks for a layered look with pizzazz.

Don't forget a few turns of your cuff to show off those statement socks!

28

THE
Quick-Change
· Artist *·*

HOW TO ACCESSORIZE
A BLACK DRESS

Slip it on and you're done—a black dress is the easiest piece in your wardrobe. Not just for formal occasions, it's perfect for commuting: You can bring heels in your bag while rocking your hippest sneaks. After hours, the creative potential abounds!

Try one of the many ways to mix up your black dress!

Bookish accessibility with a striped turtleneck layered underneath (a collared shirt also works), brooch, tights, and boots,

dressed-up elegance with a thin belt at the waist, a stunning necklace, and special shoes,

or traveling light in gladiators, a cross-body bag, and stylish hat.

29

THE
CIRCULATION
~❈DESK❈~

HOW TO ACCESSORIZE GLASSES

A *parure* is a set of jewelry worn
together. Consider creating a
parure of all types of accessories—
including jewelry, scarves, makeup,
and more—around your favorite
glasses or sunglasses. Worn as a
set, it's a considered, thoughtful
collection however you cycle
through styles.

Be inspired by these unique bespectacled looks:

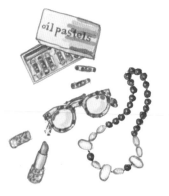

Artistic, wearing tortoiseshell frames with a peachy lip, a mod necklace that looks as if it could have been made in jewelry class, and an ever-present set of artist tools.

Adventurous, with aviators, hoop earrings, and a nod to the thrills of the Wild West with a bolo tie and all-important red cotton bandanna.

Mysterious, sporting dark glasses framed by distinctive earrings, a tiny wallet that hints of a well-traveled past, and a key ring to easily tuck into a pair of pants for a quick, quiet slip away.

Romantic, in a pair of cat-eye frames and a pearl necklace offset by architectural earrings and a stunning lip color that matches your glasses.

30

THE

MS. MIX-
⬛ a-Lot ⬛

HOW TO WEAR JEWELRY
WITH A SCARF

Arguably the two biggest
accessory MVPs, jewelry and
scarves are practically made
for each other. Separately,
they're pretty darn great,
but together, their accessory
potential packs an
unstoppable punch.

To get the most out of your scarves and jewelry . . .

. . . knot a small scarf around your neck and then layer with a choker or a brooch,

knot your scarf on the side, and then layer a necklace (or two) over the scarf,

hang a pendant from a thin scarf,

use a too-big ring to gather a scarf hung around the neck,

drape a small silk scarf over one shoulder and fasten with a brooch,

or wrap a scarf around your waist like a cummerbund and then secure with a brooch for a dash of flash.

TIP: Wrap small silk scarves around one or both of your hoop earrings for a funky update on a basic. Knot securely, and then let the scarf tails swing freely.

31

THE
-ALCHEMIST-

HOW TO MIX METALS

The alchemy of mixing silver and gold makes for one valuable sparkle. Consider the genre of your pieces as you mix those fine, shimmering filigrees with aplomb. Navy is an especially sumptuous background for this luminous combination.

Here are some ways you can combine gold and silver around your neck:

For subtle looks, choose a mix of delicate silver and gold necklaces, anchored by solid silver stud earrings.

For moderate glitter levels, try a few thick, layered chains of silver and gold, topped with structurally sound gold and crystal earrings.

For major sparkle, an over-the-top matching set of necklace and earrings are taken to untold heights with a high-impact mix of metallic necklaces.

Other places on the body, mix . . .

. . . a silver bracelet with a gold watch,

gold sunglasses with silver earrings,

or a mélange of gold and silver rings and bracelets— and look for jewelry that uses more than one metal.

32

THE
COMBO BOMB-O

HOW TO PAIR SHOES WITH A BAG

In my family, a *combo bomb-o* refers to a refreshing combination of orange juice and lemon-lime-flavored seltzer. Use that idea to jazz up your normal accessories with a remix and say "ahh" as you blend bags and shoes into something new.

The recipes for mixing your shoes and bag are simple.

There's no need to match colors—you can go with black and brown in winter,

and brown and black in summer.

Try two different colors in the same material, like this suede clutch and shoes,

or mix two different prints in similar colors.

Call to a color in a printed element with a corresponding solid,

or go for items on completely different ends of the spectrum, like a sophisticated beaded bag with a pair of kicks.

33

THE

BRIGHT FLIGHT

HOW TO ACCESSORIZE A MONOCHROMATIC LOOK

Everyone has a favorite color—it is downright uplifting to wear a head-to-toe look of your chosen hue, in a variety of textures! This high-flying outfit is created by a cerulean blue top, skirt, and wedges (all acquired on separate occasions), a necklace passed down from my mom, and a final lift, a splash of a something different, a coral belt.

Perk up your favorite colors with some of these styling ideas.

You could choose accessories, including a necklace, belt, and purse, in the same color family as your outfit, and then break it up with one contrasting hue.

Denim and a neutral toned bag are a low-key way of breaking up these maroon shirt, pants, and boots, while jewelry introduces a fresh new color.

Animal prints and stripes can really elevate a monochromatic look, like this selection of dark blues.

34

THE

KINGDOM

HOW TO ACCESSORIZE
ANIMAL PRINTS

Show your love for the animal
kingdom by sporting some skin—
imitation animal skin, of course.

Stand out in the jungle with some of these style cues.

Mix disparate animal prints by swirling in a stripe.

Leopard print shoes and a matching scarf are heightened, not hidden, by a pride of feline prints in a unifying color.

A leopard print dress with a hot red bag proves that bold colors make prints, inspired by all types of beasts, purr with pleasure.

35

THE

=Sightseer=

HOW TO ACCESSORIZE STRIPES

Stripes draw a straight line
to style. They're the perfect
neutral, incorporating a
pattern and visual interest
without requiring a detour.

I see these stripe styling tips on your horizon!

The eye is drawn up and down by a long necklace that breaks up a dress or shirt with horizontal stripes.

Gently echo a striped shirt by choosing a banded belt, skirt, and shoes.

Play with a patchwork of perpendicular stripes by pulling out a striped shirt, pants, and bag.

36

THE
LIGHT DANCE

HOW TO ACCESSORIZE METALLICS

Like sunlight flitting on the water, or the shimmer of something alluring revealing itself in your gold pan, metallics are an enticing, captivating option in any shade of sparkle.

Glisten and glint away with these approaches to incorporating metallic accessories.

Never underestimate the power of jewelry that sparkles—in endless styles ready for every season and occasion, glittery jewelry goes with everything.

Wrap a metallic belt, such as this studded version, over a metallic top. Anchor with a neutral skirt or pants, and then a shiny pair of shoes and a necklace for some extra flourishes.

A show-stopping pair of gleaming earrings, a sparkly bag, and a sequined skirt or dress are toned down with a cozy knit sweater.

A metallic belt in wide or narrow styles is an unexpected neutral when introducing flash around your waist.

37

THE
POWER FLOWER

HOW TO ACCESSORIZE FLORALS

Whether you consider
yourself a full-sun
type of bloom or
a subtle wall-
flower, floriated
fashion is always
an uplifting pick.

Gather a bouquet of floral style suggestions such as these:

Floral jewelry, like these earrings, is brought to full bloom with layers of floral tee, jacket, and scarf.

Florals on a dark background are accessorized by a bag with a light flower print and a metallic shoe.

A blossoming floral dress and cardigan are anchored by a modern, streamlined matching belt and clutch, with a strapping pair of heels that bring the look firmly into city, not country, territory.

38

THE

Passion
Fruit

HOW TO ACCESSORIZE
WITH COLOR

A well-balanced sartorial diet
includes a wide variety of color.
Choose your favorite hues for
an important daily dosage of
all your vitamins.

Create your own rainbow with some of these color styling hints.

Your toenail polish is definitely an accessory! Consider accordingly when picking out your favorite sandals.

Some rules are meant to be broken, but generally limit yourself to three separate colors. You could make it easy and choose accessories in one similar tone with a multihued outfit,

or, if you're mixing two shades (black and white are colors, too!), group like colors in "zones." A black scarf braided around your neck adds texture to a leather jacket and dark shirt, while white jeans, sneakers, and a purse keep it light on the bottom half.

A standout way of wearing fun shades is to match a colorful pair of sunglasses to your top.

39

THE

DIZZY SPELL

HOW TO MIX PRINTS

Devoted to dots? Mad about plaid? When worn at once, mixed prints are a cacophony of joy.

There is a medley of ways to mix and match prints.

Beginner level:
Add a patterned scarf
and belt to a dress,
then choose a single-
toned bag and shoes.

Intermediate level: Two
prints in different colors
come together with
accessories in colors that
speak to one of the prints.

Advanced level: An
all-over mix of prints and
tones. The only thing
that has to unite them
is your love for them!

40

THE
First Crocus

HOW TO ACCESSORIZE
IN SPRING

Start with the weather and work your way backward when it comes to getting dressed for a showery spring day. With hardworking, good-looking rain gear that you can mix and match, you'll look forward to the weather report.

TIP: Looking for even more ways to remix your spring wardrobe? Use the sash from your jacket as a hair wrap.

Try these quick ways to upgrade your average rain gear:

Swap out the sash on your trench for a scarf.

Use the sash from your trench on another raincoat.

Cinch your waterproof parka with a belt for a high-fashion take on a ready-to-get-wet getup.

When it comes to your wet-weather gear,

choose a happy umbrella,

utilitarian waterproof boots for both workday commutes and perambulating in the rain,

and a waterproof hat that will have you hoping for damp days.

41

THE
CHERRY BOMBE

HOW TO ACCESSORIZE IN SUMMER

Come in red-hot with accessories that do nothing but add to the fun in the sun.

Consider it a bathing costume instead of a swimsuit and accessorize away with your water fashions.

Wear jewelry at the pool. Here's when to try out a waist chain—turquoise and coral are classic color choices.

Buckle a belt over your one-piece suit for next-level sun bathing.

A large light scarf can be worn as a kimono in a sophisticated, dramatic way to protect from rays.

A small thin scarf can be used as a sunglasses holder in a pinch.

Don't forget your ankles and toes! An anklet or a toe ring shows that you're celebrating *every* part of your body this summer.

Honor the time of year with some seasonal jewelry. A twist of coral around the wrist, a friendship bracelet, or a few strands of seed beads remind you that summer is here.

TIP: Two things to always have in your tote through the sunny months? A bathing suit and a pretty fan. You never know when you'll need the suit, and how many times have you wished you could pull your own personal air-conditioning out of your bag?

42

THE

Granny Smith

HOW TO ACCESSORIZE IN FALL

There is something about a crisp fall day, the leaves in their golden glory, that makes a person want to reach for an outfit that reads "first day of school." It's when the superlatively stylish want to sharpen their pencils, shine their shoes, and play with layered prints and cozy textures for an autumnal A+.

Take advantage of the transitional weather by choosing the toppers you can only sport when it's not too cold or too hot.

A satchel worn with mixed herringbone patterns and a newsboy cap conveys a professor vibe.

An intellectual mix of cropped pants, ornamental top, and cheery cardigan reads master's in art history.

Moccasins, a blazer, and plaid beret convey a co-ed studying on the campus lawn next to the lake.

43

THE
Hot Toddy

HOW TO ACCESSORIZE
IN WINTER

Well-chosen accessories can turn
a basic, utilitarian wintertime coat
into a unique quotidian look.
Change up the accessories for
big-time fashion, even when
the weather insists that your
final layer stays on.

Your style can still sing in the chill.

For an additional layer of style, tug the cuffs of your shirtsleeves down so that they peek out past the sleeves of your coat. Missing a button on your jacket? Replace it with a unique button to stand out as its own piece of jewelry.

Add pins or brooches to a knit hat.

Brown polarized sunglass lenses are great for cloudy, snowy days.

Match the color of your scarf to the color of your boots for a thoughtful turn on utilitarianism.

44

THE
PINNING UP

HOW TO DRESS UP AN OUTFIT WITH ACCESSORIES

A simple tee and jeans can be taken to glamorous heights with a few strategically elevated accessory choices.

Transform a low-key outfit into something sublime!

Pin a few brooches on a shirt and weave a long chain necklace around them. (Here's a great opportunity for mixing metals! See page 80 for more tips.)

Layer a few fabulously gaudy necklaces over a very old T-shirt.

Cross a special long scarf over your body and secure with a flashy brooch.

A jazzy clutch is an instant outfit upgrader.

And divine leopard print pumps immediately elevate any occasion.

Bear in mind that perfume can be an accessory. Get into the groove of an elevated look by reserving a scent for special occasions.

45

THE ✳ PARTY IN ✳ THE VALLEY

HOW TO DRESS DOWN AN OUTFIT WITH ACCESSORIES

The most sophisticated dress can be brought back to earth with a pair of scuffed-up sneakers, while the most sparkly top can be totally approachable with something as low-key as a fanny pack.

Dress down your dressy stuff with low-key accessories.

Wear a visible bra or bralette with a strappy dress for an immediate addition of casual cool, especially with a rough leather belt.

Worn over a turtleneck with a fanny pack and a backward cap, a cocktail dress is ready to rage.

A very dressy top can be tucked into a pair of jeans or denim shorts, anchored with slick shoes and suspenders (or a pair of overalls).

46

THE
Odalisque

HOW TO ACCESSORIZE
LOUNGEWEAR

Nothing is sultrier or more languorous than running a string of pearls through your fingers as you read a book in bed. In the most private of moments, why not try a look that's a little outside of your comfort zone? It'll make your relaxed state that much more inviting.

Slide into an unwinding vibe with these decadent styling suggestions.

Why not wear your most sparkly necklace with your nightie, a scarf draped dramatically over the elbows,

a faux fur shrug or jacket tossed over flannel pajamas, finished with a fun yet cozy hat,

or a brooch nestled onto the neckline of a slip, topped with a flowing robe?

47

THE

Woman ♠ Who Will

HOW TO ACCESSORIZE
WHEN MAKING A PROFESSIONAL
FIRST IMPRESSION

You can bring positive change to the world, whatever your passions. Start with a thoughtful outfit that commands attention yet still allows your own powerful aura to shine through.

Meet success, however you define it, with these considered fashion choices.

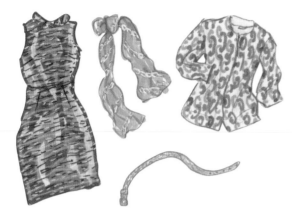 

Start with a sheath dress, layer a scarf underneath a cardigan, seal with a belt, and you'll strike an impression as a professional yet colorfully unique individual.

Select strong jewelry that will be seen if you're making a presentation to a large room.

Wear heels only if you feel comfortable walking confidently in them. Closed- and pointed-toe flats are another sleek surefire choice.

Your bag says a lot about you. Whether you choose to a carry a briefcase or a handbag, ensure that it is the most polished option you own.

48

THE

Striking Stranger

HOW TO ACCESSORIZE WHEN MAKING A PERSONAL FIRST IMPRESSION

Your unique personality already makes you stand out from the crowd! An outfit that proclaims you're ready for any spontaneous activity, combined with a ready, authentic smile, guarantees that whoever you meet will definitely want to see you again.

To make a remarkable first impression . . .

. . . choose colors and noteworthy prints that stand out from the monotony,

wear unique jewelry, such as a chain belt looped once and worn as a necklace, that gives off a self-assured vibe,

switch out the laces on a pair of sneaks for an instant recognizable upgrade,

or if you're carrying a bag, pack a large scarf that could be used as a picnic blanket in a pinch.

49

THE
Eleganza

HOW TO ACCESSORIZE
FOR A DRESS CODE

Banish dress-code confusion when
it comes to a special event and
follow these guidelines to accessorize your way to champagne
toasts and endless enjoyment.

DID YOU KNOW?
Van Cleef & Arpels created the
minaudière, a small handbag
perfect for formal occasions,
in 1933 after seeing socialite
Florence Gould carry her
cosmetics and lighter in a
Lucky Strike cigarette tin.

Decode the dress code with some of these suggestions.

For "come as you are" casual, a statement necklace adds levity.

For business and business casual, err on the side of streamlined, heeding Coco Chanel's advice to take off one accessory before leaving the house.

For a dressy event such as an outdoor wedding, choose wedges or dressier sandals for walking across a lawn or beach.

For festive, seasonal celebrations, sequins, satin, and velvet are always welcome on the guest list. Sprinkle with sparkly flourishes like a bowtie and glittery tights.

For cocktail parties, take a turn in a festive monochromatic look by pairing an elegant top, pants, and shoes in similar tones with an elegant clutch.

For black-tie events, reach for a few lavish embellishments you may rarely have a chance to wear, like opulent jewelry, a handsome hair accessory, and an extravagantly embellished purse.

THE
Everlasting Bliss

HOW TO ACCESSORIZE
ACCORDING TO MOOD

People have been wearing accessories for spiritual, religious, or amuletic (to protect the wearer from harm) reasons for millennia. You may already own something that makes you feel safe, loved, or joyous—tap into your subconscious and wear those pieces with purpose!

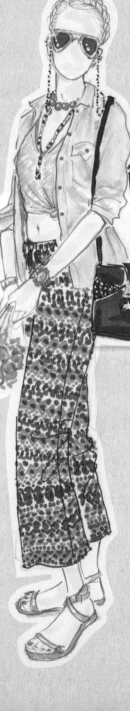

Here are just a few of the many ways to adorn and adore yourself with a special accessory:

Collect pieces featuring your guardian animal. Some unexpected places to wear your favorite species could be on socks or a scarf. Wear them when you want to tap into your intuition.

Jewelry made from animal parts, real or imitation, is a protective practice dating back thousands of years. Wear them when you want to feel powerful.

Eyes are a significant symbol seen in many cultures. Wearing them, such as on a handbag or a pair of earrings, is thought to offer immunity from harm.

Many believe that crystals and minerals have healing powers. Amber, obsidian, quartz, black tourmaline, and turquoise are just some. Wear with jewelry, on a belt, or simply keep a stone in your pocket when you want to feel contentment.

Prayer beads take many forms, but they all are used as tools for connecting with a higher power.

Accessories that are engraved or embroidered, or even a tattoo with a special or secret message, can be uniquely important for the wearer. Wear for a constant reminder of your loves and how you are loved.

HISTORICAL TIMELINE

30,000 BC:
Remains discovered from this time show that many humans wore jewelry made from simple beads, while huntsmen wore pendants crafted from bone and teeth. The continent of Africa is where early humans first made and wore jewelry.

23,000 BC:
In a Chinese book called the *Shu-king* scribed from this time, a court writer describes the gift sent from an inferior king as "strings of pearls not quite round."

2500 BC:
Estimated creation date of some of the oldest known gold jewelry, found in the tombs of Ur in Mesopotamia for Queen Pu-abi.

2000–1300 BC:
The Egyptians innovate on many levels of accessories. Specialized kinds of footwear are developed after going outside barefoot comes to be viewed as improper. Dangling earrings appear, first worn only by women. A clasp for bracelets and necklaces is invented. All members of society wear some type of jewelry, while the royalty sports

incredibly elaborate pieces that are intended to be buried with them at death as gifts to the afterworld.

1700–1100 BC:
Approximate date for the original creation of the *Rig Veda*, a holy Hindu text written in ancient India. One section describes the Hindu god Krishna discovering pearls in the sea to give to his daughter on her wedding day.

1800–500 BC:
During the Bronze and Iron Ages of Western Europe, the Celts of Ireland pioneer lunulae,

or "little moons," on brooches, scarf pins, and more.

900–400 BC:

In Ancient Greece and Rome, small pouches dangle from the waist, serving as early purses. The smaller the bag, the higher the indication of social status. The purse frequently is used as a symbol of the womb, worn by the Roman goddess of fertility Uberitas.

322 BC:

Alexander the Great's military spoils in Egypt and Western Asia on behalf of the Roman Empire include gold, new types of gemstones and designs, and jewelry-making techniques.

27 BC:

The Roman imperial period sees gold once again used for jewelry, after the metal was previously consumed by military expenses. Around this time, the Roman general Vitellius allegedly sells one of his mother's pearl earrings to finance an entire military campaign.

529 AD:

Through the *Code of Justinian*, all members of Byzantium have the right to wear a gold ring, while pearls, emeralds, and sapphires are reserved solely for the emperor to wear.

ELEVENTH CENTURY:

Bishop of Rennes in Brittany writes the *Book of Stones*, which outlines how to use and wear precious stones for medicinal and protective purposes. Jewels are set with open backs to allow direct contact on skin and are drilled through the middle so that more powers can be released.

1204:

Constantinople is sacked by crusaders on their way to the Holy Land. Jewels, church ornaments, and relics are carried back west, indelibly influencing the decorative arts of medieval Europe and flooding the market with plundered metalwork, new ideas, and precious metals.

THIRTEENTH CENTURY:

Accessories that serve both necessity (such as keeping warm in freezing palaces) and style grow. Women wear a wimple, which covers the throat and conveniently helps them keep warm, and there is demand for artificial flowers, silk, and sequins (which were known in ancient Egypt) adapted for dress and hats. Women wear pouches that are attached to a belt. Eyebrows and hairlines are plucked to make a person's forehead appear larger in order to convey an image of higher status.

EARLY FOURTEENTH CENTURY:

Europeans finally master gem-cutting techniques that have been practiced for centuries in India and Persia. Bruges, Belgium, becomes the epicenter of diamond cutting in Europe.

LATE FOURTEENTH CENTURY:

The fashion of wearing bulky medieval head-dresses falls by the wayside as European women start to carefully arrange their hair and decorate their long strands with strings of pearls and jewels.

1492:

Columbus lands in the Americas, seizing upon gold, silver, and emeralds. These precious elements are brutally plundered from local inhabitants before sources for the precious materials are located and actively mined, such as emeralds in what is now the country of Colombia. Other European explorers

discover Native Americans across the continent wearing pearls. In Central America, Spanish colonizers force slaves to dive for pearls.

1498:

Vasco da Gama forges a route to India, a country that quickly becomes the main supplier of diamonds for Europeans.

SIXTEENTH CENTURY:

Accessories grow to be indelibly intertwined with the economic, cultural, and political system. Precious jewels and jewelry are frequently included in bank loans. Artists in Italy, including Botticelli and Donatello, train as goldsmiths. King Francis I of France invents the concept of "crown jewels" by declaring at least eight pieces to be inalienable heirlooms of French kings.

SEVENTEENTH CENTURY:

The growth of a prosperous middle class leads to the adoption of diamond wearing by the bourgeoisie. Botany, bows, and flourishes with excessive decoration define the accessories of this period, leading to the rococo style, which originates in Paris.

EIGHTEENTH CENTURY:

In France under the reign of Louis XV, women decorate their hair with bunches of artificial flowers and wear a choker around the neck based on the fashion of the king's most notorious mistress, Madame de Pompadour. Straw hats are in vogue for a "rustic" nod to shepherdesses, and it is briefly fashionable to wear false eyebrows made from mouse fur. In Venice, Italy, Venetians wear half masks in nice weather, and full masks to cover the face in windy weather.

1720:

Soon after the brilliant cut diamond appears in jewelry making, Indian diamond mines are completely depleted. Diamond mines in Brazil are discovered in this year.

1785:

"The Diamond Necklace Affair" leads to revolutionary discontent and the eventual revolution of France. Queen Marie Antoinette, in the court of King Louis XVI, is implicated to have been part of a fraud that involves an extravagantly expensive diamond necklace.

EARLY NINETEENTH CENTURY:

Accessory styles for women in the early part of this century are sweetly feminine in order to reflect a man's creditworthiness and acumen. Ladies carry dainty props and wear clothing which restricts movement, such as shawls, bonnets, and bone stays. These items act as a deliberate foil to the masculine archetype. Women are not in charge of their own finances, and the less a woman carries, the more it conveys her status as someone who has someone else to carry her possessions. Women's

"purses" are essentially pouches called "reticules" which hold rouge and calling cards.

1822:

John Hetherington, a London haberdasher, incites a riot when he wears a new tall hat of his design while walking down the street. He is charged with "inciting a breach of the peace."

MID-NINETEENTH CENTURY:

The explosion of industry and worldwide expansion leads to steel jewelry in England, a chain-making machine patented in 1859, clip-on earrings manufactured in the 1860s, and a revival of ancient jewelry design forms with archeological discoveries.

1865:

Slavery is abolished in the United States. Before this, new colonies had laws called "sumptuary laws" that dictated how free and enslaved black women could dress, including the requirement that they must cover their hair with a head wrap. Though wearing a head wrap is often considered a source of shame at this time, for free black Creole women living in Louisiana, wearing head wraps, which they decorate with ribbon, feathers, and jewels, is a fashionable act of rebellion.

1870S:

With the advent of travel, both through the unfolding of railroads and transatlantic routes, along with the spread of the British Empire, the carpetbag becomes an integral part of the voyage. Carpetbags not only allow travelers to keep all their items in a handheld tote, but also can be opened and used as a blanket on long overnight trips. Although originally used by men, they are adopted by women and later made iconic by the British character Mary Poppins. In addition, the invention of the automobile and the bicycle usher in a new category of fashion accessories geared toward biking and motoring.

1893:

Whitcomb L. Judson invents the zipper. When the handbag framers of Manhattan go on strike in 1923, manufacturers start to put zippers on handbags to sidestep the strikers.

1900:

Dog collar necklaces become popular after Queen Alexandra, Princess of Wales, wears them to cover a scar on her neck.

1900:

As women fight for independence, financially, politically, and culturally, the first appearance of the word *handbag* appears. No longer carrying bags that are simply for frivolities, bags begin to clasp shut, protecting women's new access to cash and financial autonomy, that "snap" signifying independence.

1903:

The American Suffragist movement, which successfully campaigned for women's right to vote through the Nineteenth Amendment, turns to over-the-shoulder bags so that both hands could be free to carry protest signs.

1908:

A young Harry Winston spies a green ring in the window of a pawn shop and buys it for 25 cents. He sells this two-karat emerald two days later for $800. A genius with precious stones, he will later be known to keep spectacular specimens in his jacket pocket.

1910:

Paul Poiret and Mariano Fortuny, fashion designers popular at the turn of the twentieth century, design dresses without corsets, ushering in a new silhouette and encouraging stylish women to accessorize with more brooches, long necklaces, and head ornaments.

1910:
Jeanne Toussaint joins Cartier at the age of twenty-three, becoming one of the first female designers at a jewelry house, creating an influential line of accessories, handbags, makeup cases, and jewelry.

1922:
The discovery of King Tut's tomb leads to an explosion of Egyptian-inspired styles. The influential choreographer Sergei Diaghilev and his Ballet Russes company, which frequently partners with artists, composers, and designers such as Pablo Picasso, Igor Stravinsky, and Coco Chanel, heralds this "Tutmania" with Egyptian-influenced costumes. Jewelry houses introduce baubles that feature the sphinx, scarab, and other Egyptian icons.

1920S:
The shedding of antiquated values is symbolized by many women (referred to as "flappers")

adopting head-turning new fashions. The waists of their dresses are dropped, their sleeves are chopped, and their formal gloves are shed for accessories, such as long opera-length necklaces and structured clutches which showcase the nouveau decorative arts. Diamond bracelets are tantalizingly called "service stripes" as a reference to one's "impermanent liaisons," and wearing them in multiples is particularly popular. By 1926 the cloche has taken over Europe, a hat that pairs perfectly with the modish trend of wearing the hair in a short bob style.

1930S:
A decade after beauty maven Helena Rubinstein pioneers the mixing of fine gems with dime-store "junk," women's fashion designers Coco Chanel and Elsa Schiaparelli popularize the practice of high-low fashion by pairing costume jewelry with genuine jewels, mixing traditional "day"

and "night" decoration for a groundbreaking new way of approaching sartorial rules.

1930:
The film *Romance* is released. Costume designer Adrian designs a hat for Greta Garbo's character that will influence millinery styles for the next decade. Adrian grows to renown after dressing icons such as Joan Crawford, and will go on to pioneer the practice of designing costume jewelry based on the pieces used on camera.

1932:
The innovative jewelry designer Suzanne Belperron takes the head design job at the house of Parisian gem dealer Bernard Herz. She considers her work so original she chooses not to sign any of her pieces, believing their uniqueness is the only signature necessary. Mr. Herz, who is of Jewish origin, is protected for

years by Ms. Belperron from the Nazi Gestapo. When they are both arrested in 1942, she swallows the pages of his client address book one by one in order to protect her boss and their clients. Mr. Herz is taken to the concentration camp Auschwitz, in Poland, and Ms. Belperron joins the resistance movement against the Nazis while remaining in Paris through the war.

1940S:

While men are at war, American women come out in droves to keep the work force running. Women's fashion is liberated with comfortable shoes, handbags that leave both hands free, and adaptations of men's styles.

1947:

Following the period of austerity during both world wars, Christian Dior shocks the style scene by unveiling his "New Look," which features a low neckline, nipped waist, and voluminous skirt. Necklaces evolve into a bib style to fit with the new necklines.

1950S:

The enfranchisement of women during the '30s and '40s swings the opposite way as society, fearful of a nuclear threat and fatigued of war, reinforces traditional gender roles. Women, in their "rightful" place at the home, are encouraged to invest in good handbags, shoes, and gloves.

1953:

Ann Lowe, an African American fashion designer who, rarely photographed but almost always shown wearing a black hat and fashionable eyeglasses to aid her failing eyesight, designs the wedding dress future First Lady Jacqueline Bouvier wears when she marries Senator John F. Kennedy in this year. Ms. Lowe does not receive public credit for this work at the time.

1956:

Grace Kelly hides her pregnancy with the Prince of Monaco with an Hermès bag. It is renamed "the Kelly" after her.

1960S:

The "Youthquake" originates in London and spreads a new age of counterculturist values. The "Swinging Sixties" are named after the mod shoulder bags, pioneered by young designers like Mary Quant, which swing from the shoulders.

1962:

Bonnie Cashin becomes a designer at Coach, creating pared-down, streamlined bags that are hugely influential for the American leather goods purveyor. She famously says that we should "banish the word *match*," instead designing simple leather bag forms that can be mixed and matched together or worn separately.

1967:
The release of the film *Bonnie and Clyde* doubles the sales of berets in America.

1970S:
Uncertainty in world events leads to a rise in value placed on homemade goods and "anti" design. "Ethnic" fashion appropriated from oppressed nations is also popular.

1977:
Studio 54 opens. While its doors are open for only two years, the impact of its clubgoers' styles is deeply felt for a long time—the Dionysian elements of excess and celebration draw out styles of fetishism, leopard prints, platforms, and leather in accessories.

1980S:
A dichotomy emerges between antiquated images of women's success (such as UK prime minister Margaret Thatcher's constantly present Salvatore Ferragamo purse) and women breaking the "glass ceiling" in men's-style suiting and briefcases. Donna Karan designs a woman's briefcase that features a small hidden feminine purse, addressing the "day to night" dressing challenge.

1981:
Actress Joan Collins is offered a role on the then struggling soap opera *Dynasty*. She catapults the show to wide commercial success while sporting an enviable mix of outrageously extravagant accessories.

1985:
Miuccia Prada, at the helm of her family's long-running leather goods firm, designs a backpack out of nylon. Created in response to the threat of global warming and a world recession, the minimal design of this bag belies its indelible influence, ushering in a new era of accessory styles that reflect growing global threats.

1990:
Risk becomes a major component of fashion. Bags are hung across the body for safety, while ripstop and bulletproof fabrics fabricate a new style of minimalist grunge.

2000S:
Handbags become a seasonal element with fashion shows and grow into a marker of class status. Brands practice "seeding"—sending bags, gratis, to celebrities so that they will be photographed by paparazzi carrying them.

2018 AND BEYOND:
Accessories are the true mass-market fashion object, whether purchased for a pretty penny, gifted by a family member, or handmade. They connect cultures and prove that an appreciation for accessories is most definitely one size fits all!

READING LIST

The following books provided information, inspiration, and delight about accessories throughout the process of working on this book.

Amphlett, Hilda. *Hats: A History of Fashion in Headwear.* Dover Publications, 2003.

Berger, Barbara, Harrice Simons Miller, and Pablo Esteva. *Fashion Jewelry: The Collection of Barbara Berger.* Assouline Publishing, 2013.

Corbett, Patricia, Ward Landrigan, and Nico Landrigan. *Jewelry by Suzanne Belperron.* Thames & Hudson Ltd., 2015.

Cox, Caroline. *The Handbag: An Illustrated History.* Collins Design, 2007.

Peacock, Hudson. *Fashion Accessories: The Complete 20th Century Sourcebook.* Thames & Hudson Ltd., 2000.

Phillips, Clare. *Jewelry: From Antiquity to the Present.* Thames & Hudson Ltd., 1996.

Price, Candy Pratt, Jessica Glasscock, and Art Tavee. *American Fashion Accessories: Council of Fashion Designers of America.* Assouline Publishing, 2008.

Rivers, Joan. *Jewelry by Joan Rivers.* Abbeville Press Inc., 1995.

Tait, Hugh. *7000 Years of Jewelry.* Firefly Books Ltd., 2008.

ACKNOWLEDGMENTS

This book would not be possible without the encouraging, inspiring work done by my editor Deanne Katz, and the rest of the Chronicle Books team: Jennifer Tolo Pierce, Marie Oishi, Lindsay Sablosky, Freesia Blizard, and Alexandra Brown. With gratitude, I'd like to thank my friends for endlessly stoking the collective fires of creativity. Thank you to Ashlea and Laura, for help with the cover. Ruth and Tracey, for important literature and inspiration. Whitney, whose thoughtful, loving presence sustained me. My brother, whose words of encouragement and acts of kindness kept me moving. My dad, for giving me strength and stability. My mom, who offered a keen set of second eyes and an open closet (as long as I returned everything). And last but not least, thank you to my family: my aunts, uncles, cousins, grandparents, all the people whose names we still say out loud and all those we have long forgotten. While creating this book, I learned that accessories are a door through which we access our collective histories. The act of choosing, wearing, and appreciating accessories encircles us, simultaneously anchoring us to our past while handing us the tools to assist in divining a bright future. May we honor ourselves through the sacred art of adornment, decorating our bodies in a world where we all recognize and celebrate one another's unique expressions, under the surface of which, of course, we are all one.